This workbook belongs to:

....

Date Started: **Date Finished:**

⭐ **Look What I Did** ⭐

Mark your progress as you complete each excercise.

Lessons

1	2	3	4	5
6	7	8	9	10

From A to Z

WELCOMES YOU TO

A Math Retreat

(color me)

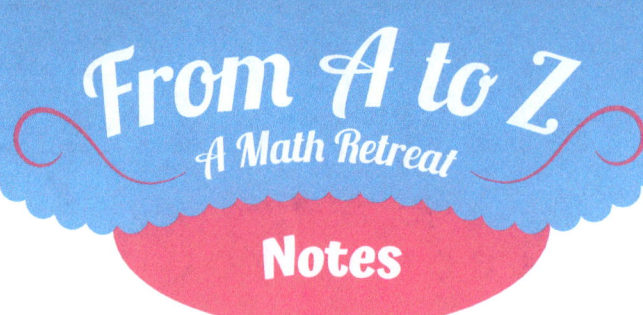

Name: _____

Date: _____

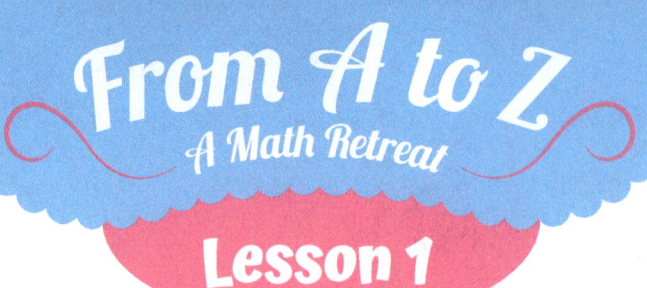

Lesson 1

✏ Count and Add

Count each item in the group, then add the groups together. An example has been done for you.

🟢🟢🟢 + 🔴🔴 = (3) + (2) = [5]

🫖🫖 + 🫖🫖 = (2) + (2) = [4]

🦎🦎🦎🦎🦎🦎🦎 + 🦎🦎🦎 = (7) + (3) = [10]

4

🖊🖊🖊🖊🖊 + 🖊🖊🖊 = ⬤5 + ⬤3 = ▢8

🧦🧦🧦 + 🧦🧦🧦🧦🧦🧦🧦 = ⬤3 + ⬤7 = ▢10

👟👟👟👟 + 👟👟👟 = ⬤4 + ⬤3 = ▢7

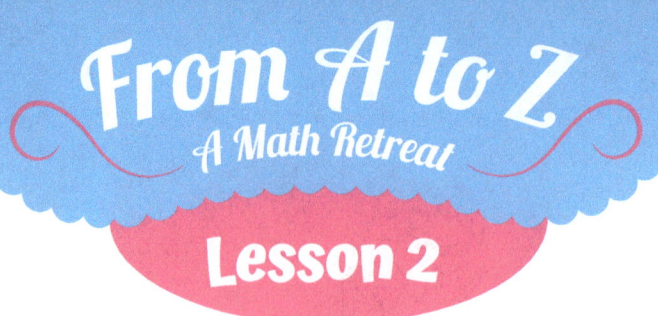

Lesson 2

✏️ **Count and Add**

Count each item in the group, then add the groups together. An example has been done for you.

Amber has one orange book and Tammie has six blue books. How many books do they have in all?

📕 + 📘📘📘📘📘📘 = ⑦ + ⑥ = 7

Zack has six pink cups and Fran has four yellow cups. How many cups do they have altogether?

🥤🥤🥤🥤🥤 + 🥤🥤🥤🥤 = ⑤ + ④ = 9

Hailey has two purple flowers. David has six red flowers. How many flowers do they have in total?

Xavier has seven gold spoons and Quinn has four silver spoons. How many spoons are there altogether?

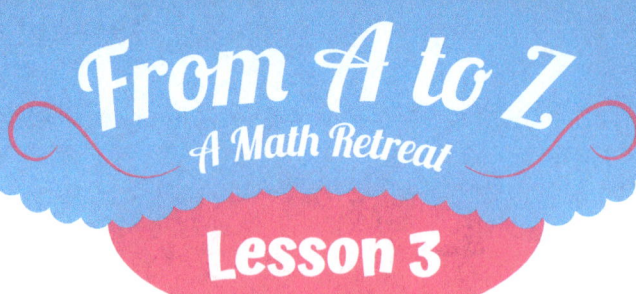

Lesson 3

✏️ Addition Practice

Solve the addition problems.

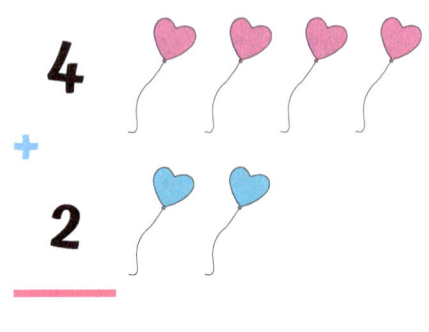

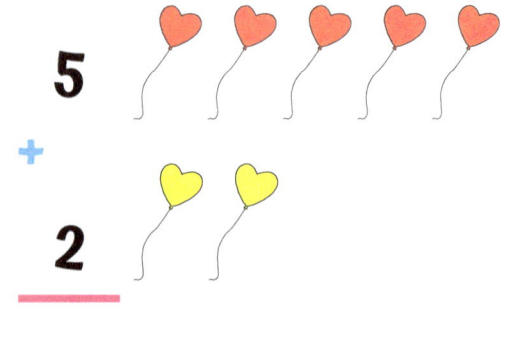

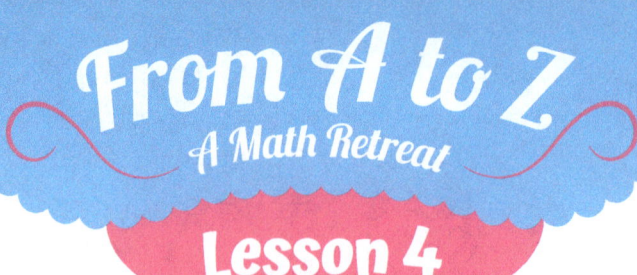

Lesson 4

✏️ Addition Practice

Solve the addition problems.

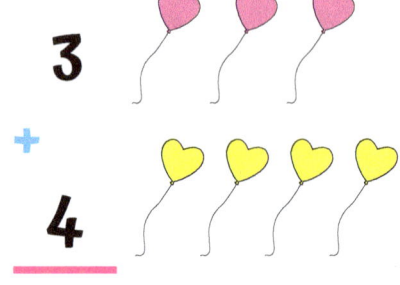

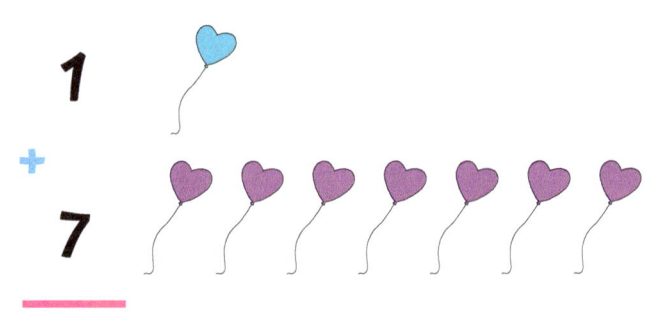
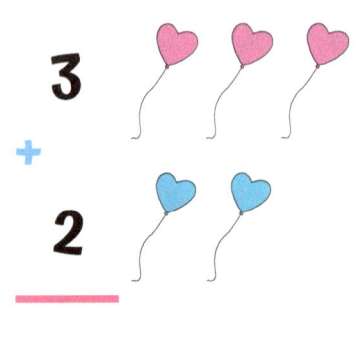
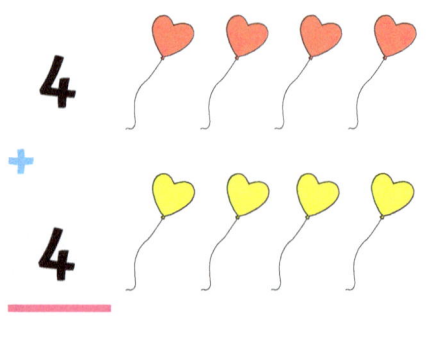

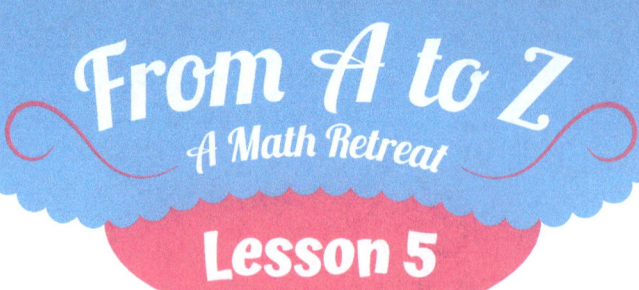

Lesson 5

✏️ **Which Equal 5?**

Color in the stars that have an answer of 5

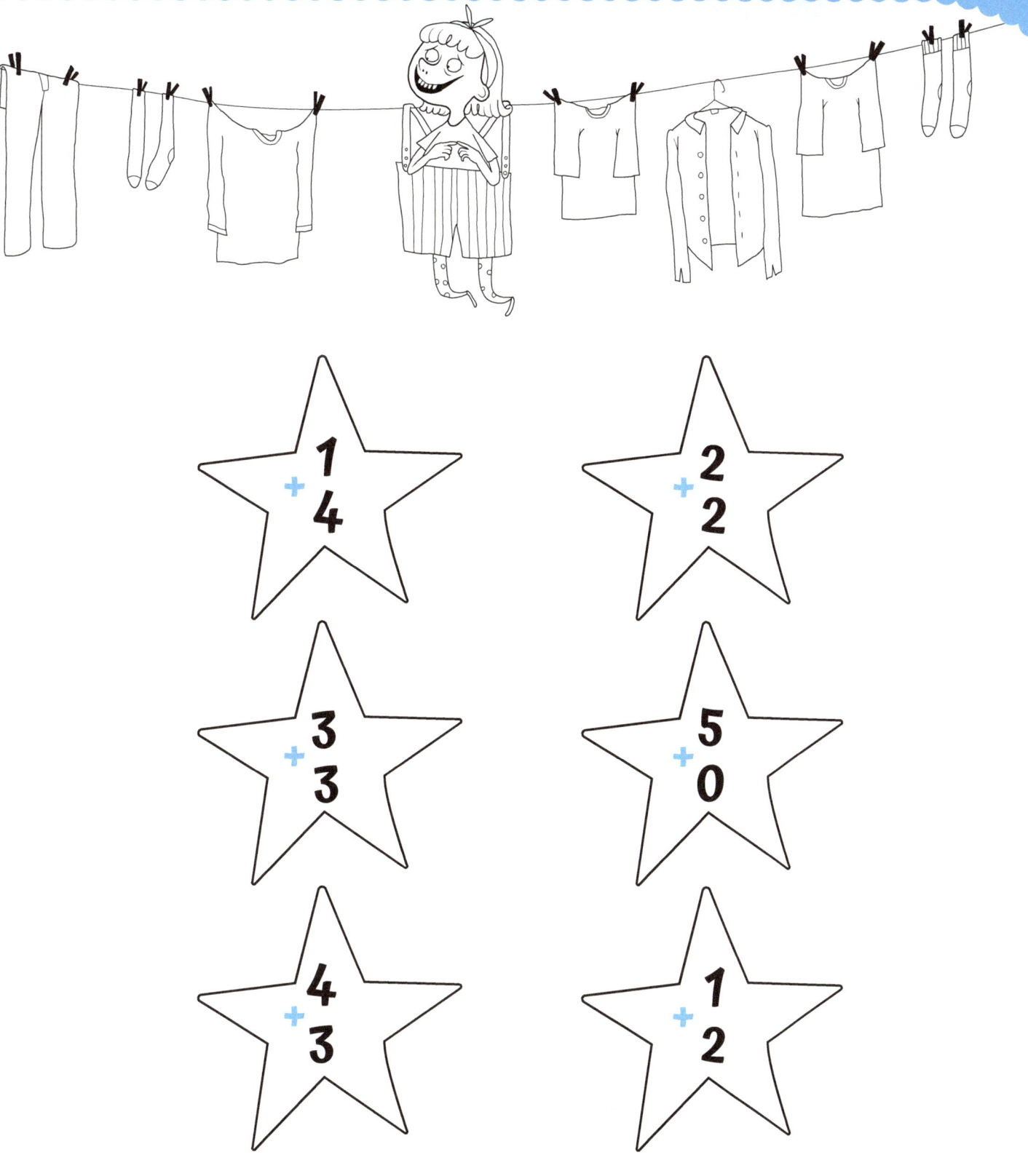

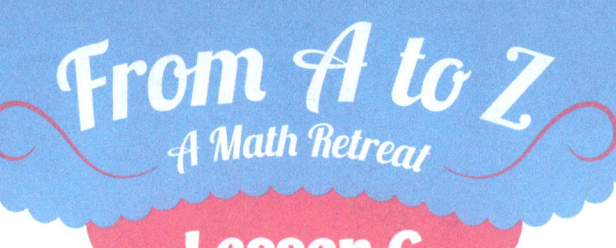

Lesson 6

Which Equal 5?

Color in the stars that have an answer of 5

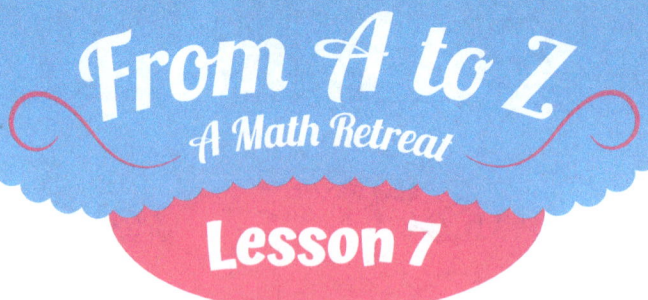

Lesson 7

✏️ What's the Answer?

Color in the correct answer for each problem shown.

🍪🍪 + 🔵 = ?

| 3 | 2 | 4 |

🍉🍉 + 🍉🍉🍉🍉🍉🍉 = ?

| 6 | 8 | 7 |

| 7 | 6 | 5 |

| 4 | 6 | 5 |

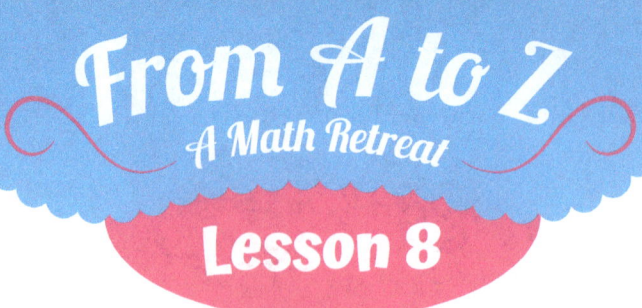

Lesson 8

✏️ What's the Answer?

Color in the correct answer for each problem shown.

🍕 + 🍕🍕🍕 = ?

| 2 | 3 | 4 |

🍩🍩 + 🍩🍩 = ?

| 2 | 1 | 4 |

4 + 5 = ?

| 9 | 7 | 8 |

5 + 2 = ?

| 6 | 8 | 7 |

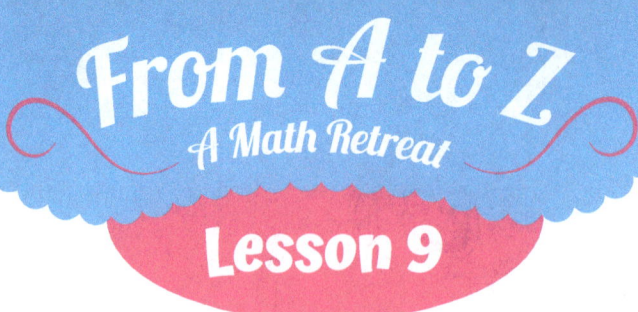

Lesson 9

✍ **Solve the riddle**

What does Penelope love to be?

....
 4   2   7   5   10   6   9   7

- C) 5+5
- R) 5+4
- I) 3+2
- N) 5+2
- A) 3+1
- U) 1+1
- O) 4+2

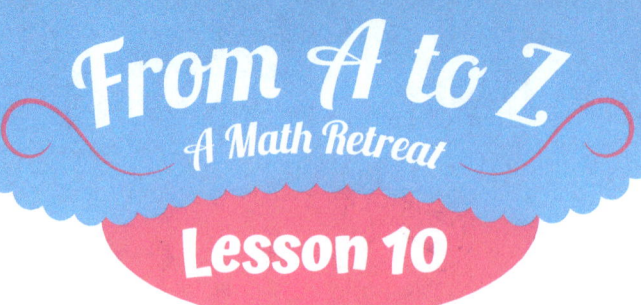

Lesson 10

✏️ **Solve the riddle**

What sport does Chris play?

....
  5   2   7   7   3   6

C 5 + 5

R 5 + 4

S 1 + 1

O 4 + 2

Congratulations! You're an addition master!

You successfully completed your first full week of the Jumbo Math lessons.

Go reward yourself with some relaxation time before you start on next week's Math activities.

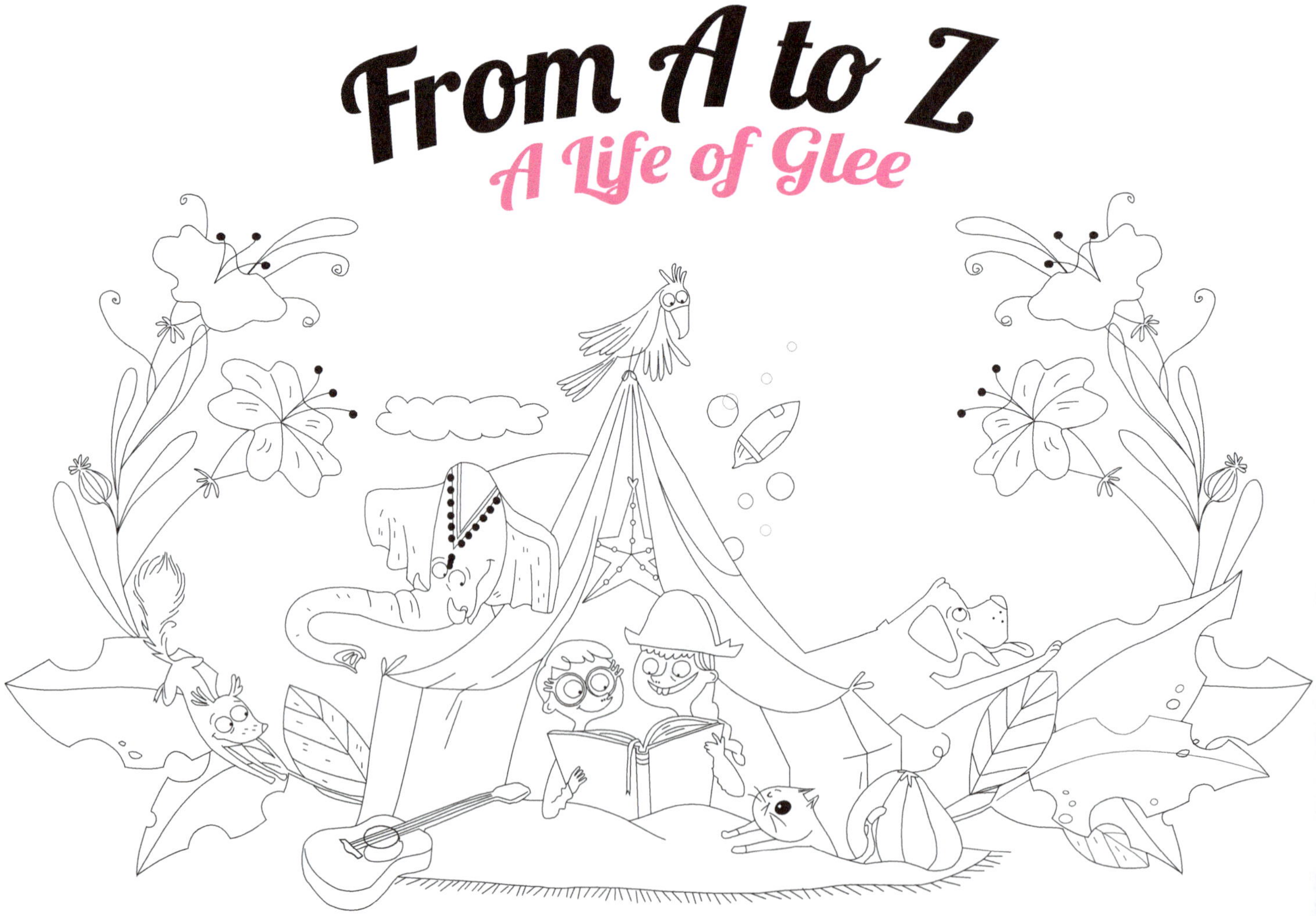

This workbook belongs to:

....

Date Started: .... **Date Finished:** ....

⭐ Look What I Did ⭐

Mark your progress as you complete each excercise.

Lessons

1	2	3	4	5
6	7	8		

From A to Z
WELCOMES YOU TO
A Math Retreat

(color me)

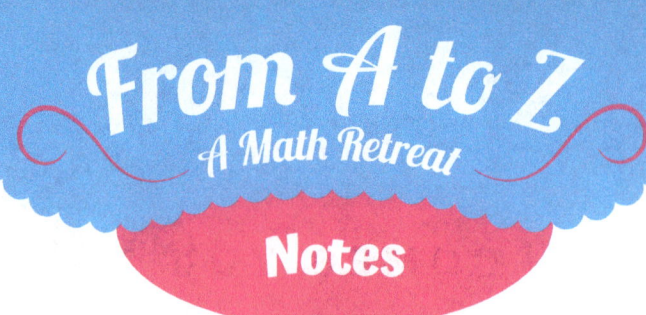

Name: _____

Date: _____

Lesson 1

 **Number Hunt**

Trace the number

1	1 1 1 1 1 1 1
one	one one one

2	2 2 2 2 2
two	two two two

3 3 3 3 3 3

three three three

4 4 4 4 4 4

four four four

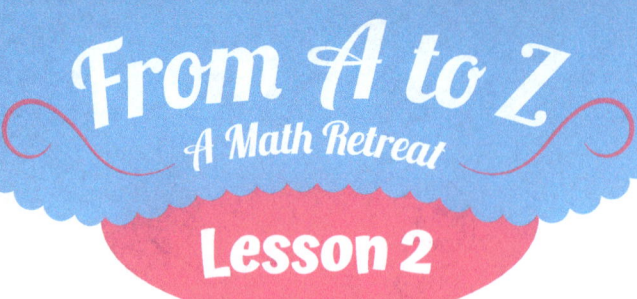

Lesson 2

Trace the number

5 — 5 5 5 5 5

five — five five five

6 — 6 6 6 6 6

Six — Six Six Six Six

7 7 7 7 7 7

seven seven seven

8 8 8 8 8 8

eight eight eight

Lesson 3

✎ **Number Hunt**

Trace the number

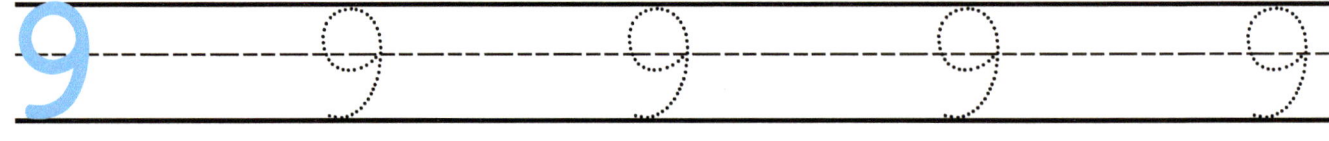

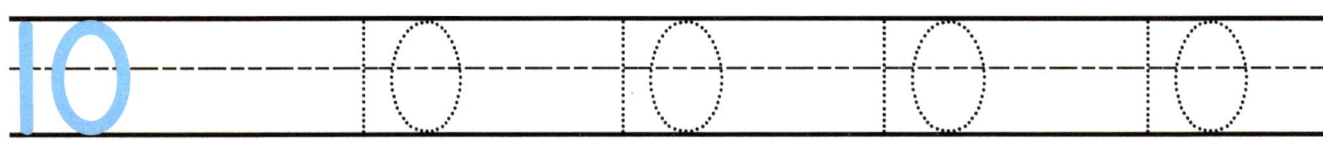

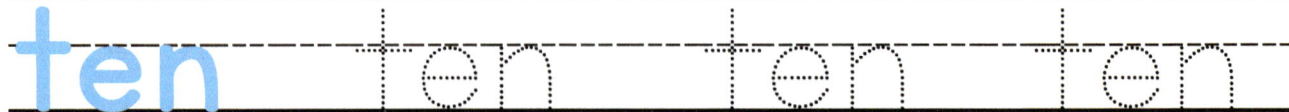

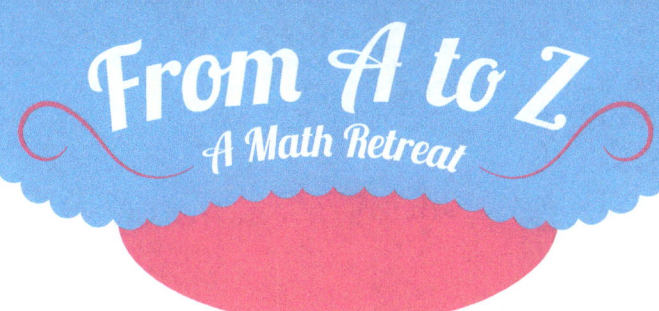

Number Match

Draw a line to match each number with it's name.

1	Ten
7	Four
3	Six
8	One
2	Five
4	Three
9	Eight
5	Two
10	Seven
6	Nine

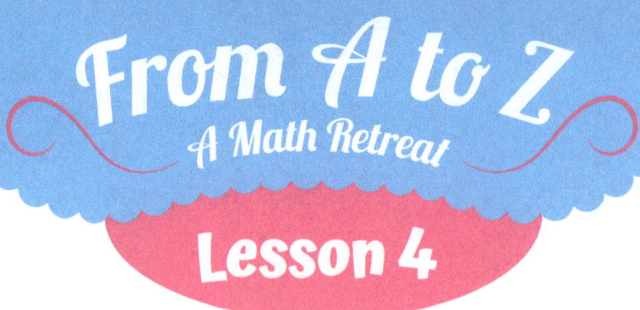

Lesson 4

✏️ **Draw One More**

Count how many items are in each picture. Draw one more item in each group. Count how many items are in each group again.

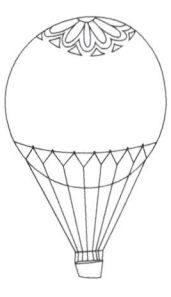 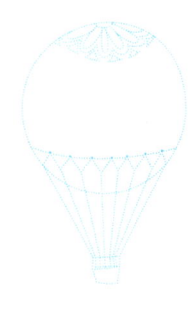 

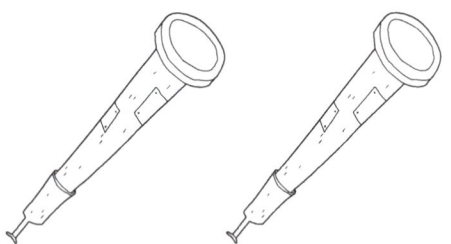 

 Mice

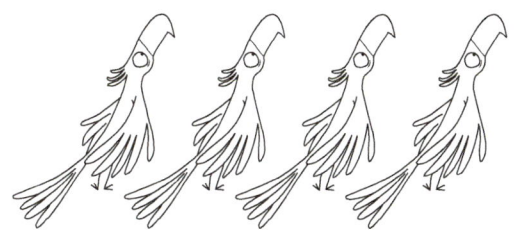
 Parrots

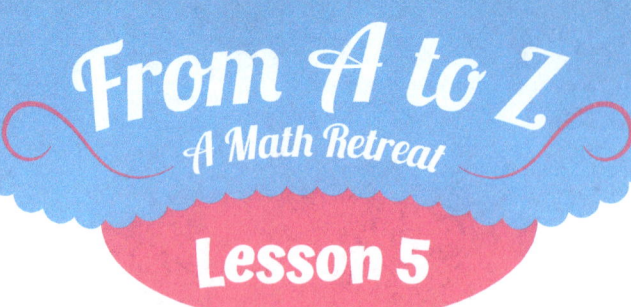

Lesson 5

✏️ **Draw One More**

Count how many items are in each picture. Draw one more item in each group. Count how many items are in each group again.

    Pumpkings

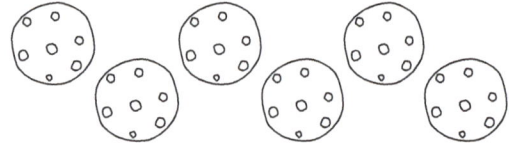    Cookies

    Cakes

 Frogs

 Umbrellas

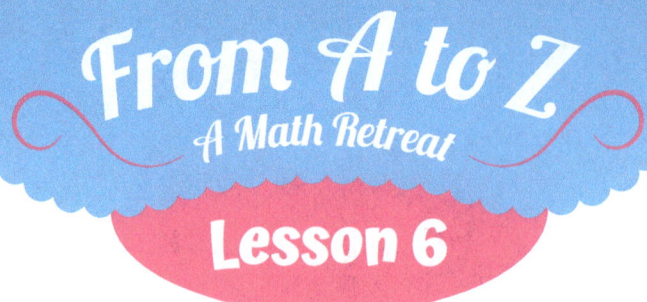

Lesson 6

✏️ Count the Number

Count how many items are in each box. Then circle the correct number for your answer.

3
(4) 2

9
4   6

3
5   1

4
10 1

5
6 3

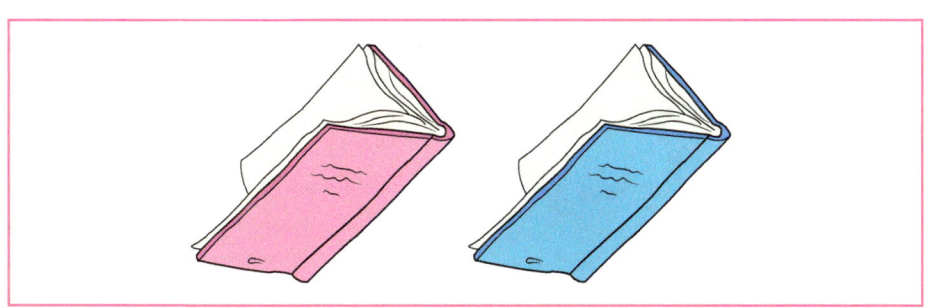

4
2 8

From A to Z
A Math Retreat
Lesson 7

✏️ **Draw the Number**

Draw the correct number of each item.

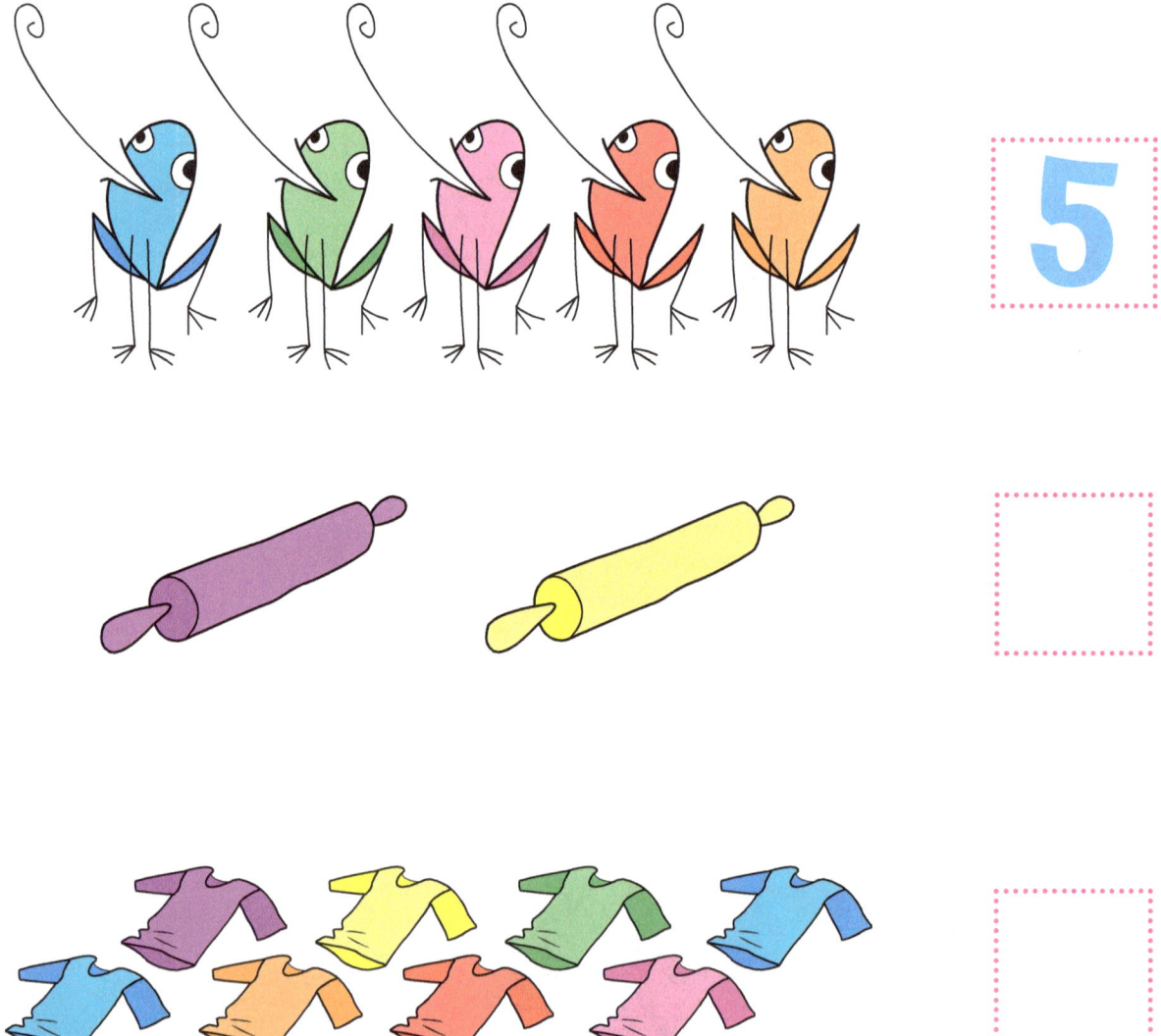

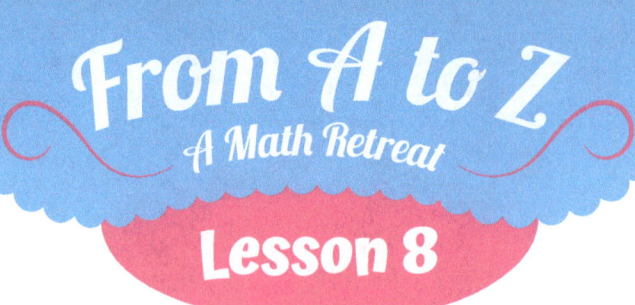

Lesson 8

✏ Draw the Number

Draw the correct number of each item.

| 2 | 5 | 6 |

| 5 | 8 | 7 |

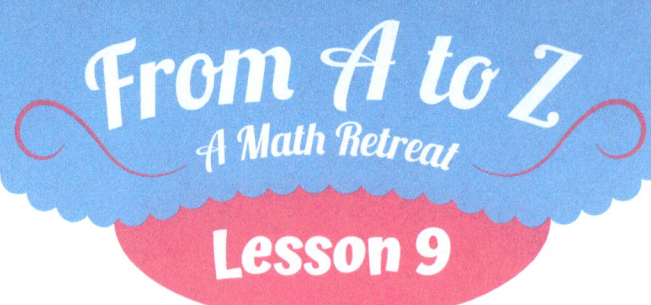

Lesson 9

✎ Word Search

Find each number in the word search.

```
E  V  I  F  X
E  E  R  H  T
N  T  W  O  J
O  N  N  J  N
N  F  O  U  R
```

One Two Three Four Five

Match the Number

Find each number in the word search.

Three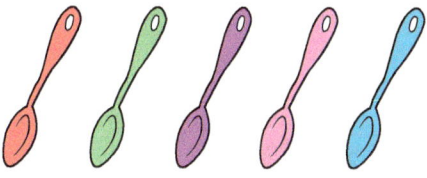

One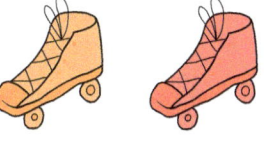

Two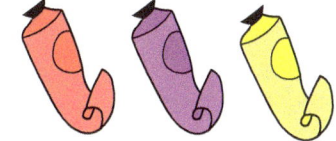

Five

Four

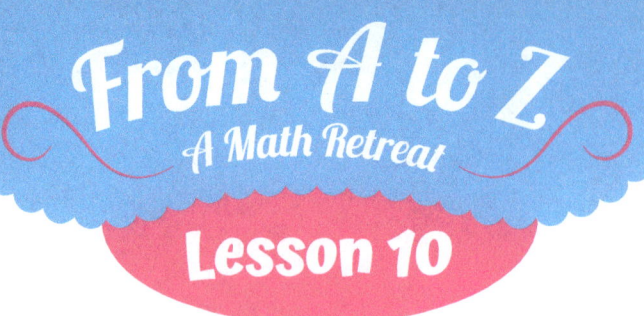

Lesson 10

✏️ Color by Number

Color the picture using the code below.

1 = Yellow 2 = Black 3 = Blue 4 = White 5 = Orange
6 = Green 7 = Red 8 = Purple 9 = Brown 10 = Pink

1 = Yellow   2 = Black   3 = Blue   4 = White   5 = Orange

6 = Green   7 = Red   8 = Purple   9 = Brown   10 = Pink

Congratulations! You're a math magician!

You successfully completed your second week of the Jumbo Math lessons.

Go reward yourself with some relaxation time before you start on next week's Math activities.

From A to Z
A Life of Glee

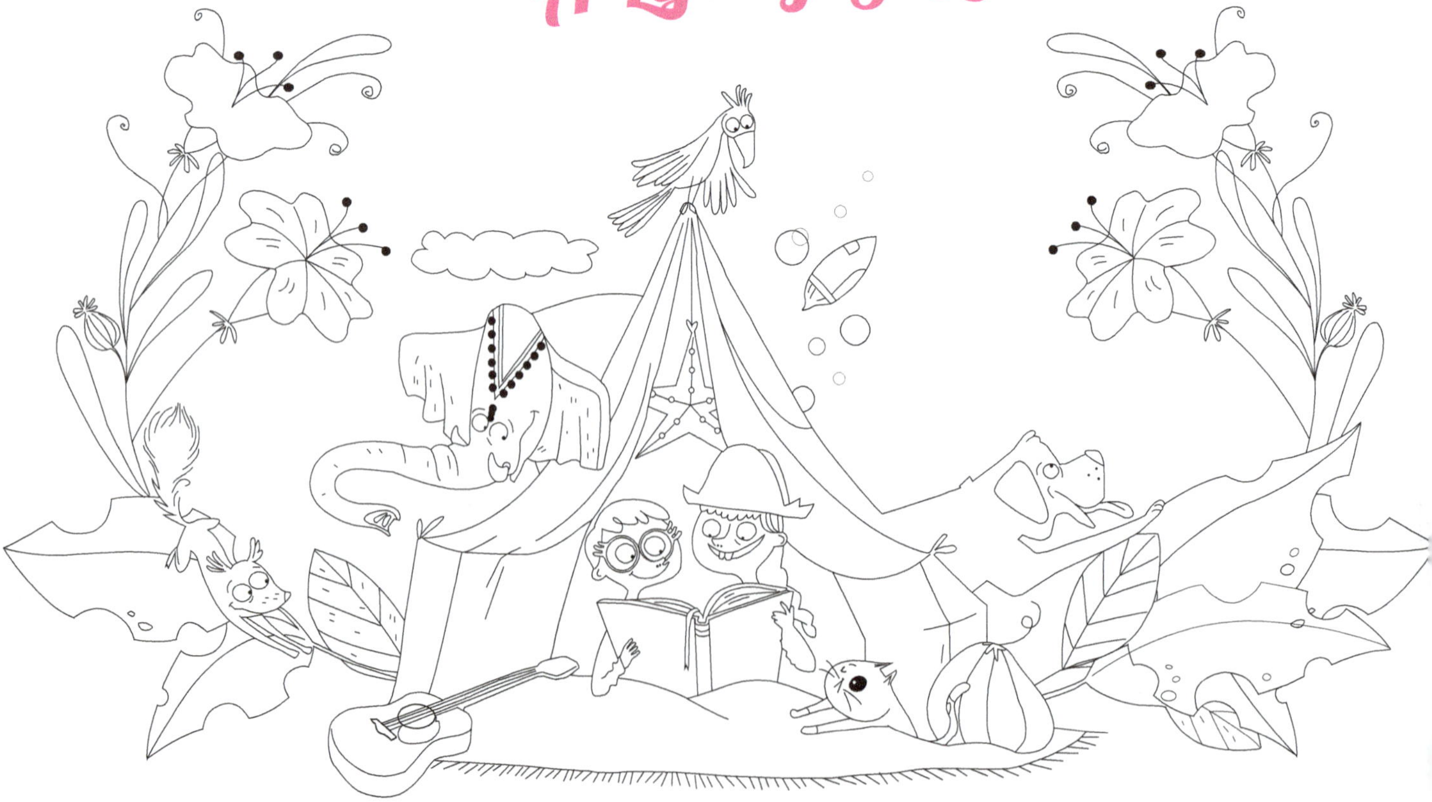

This workbook belongs to:

....

Date Started: .... **Date Finished:** ....

⭐ Look What I Did ⭐

Mark your progress as you complete each excercise.

Lessons

1	2	3	4	5
6	7	8	9	10

From A to Z
WELCOMES YOU TO
A Math Retreat

(color me)

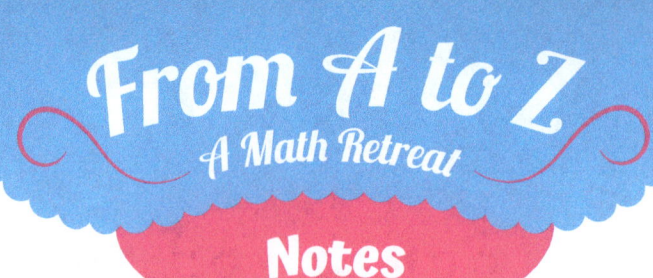

Notes

Name: _____
Date: _____

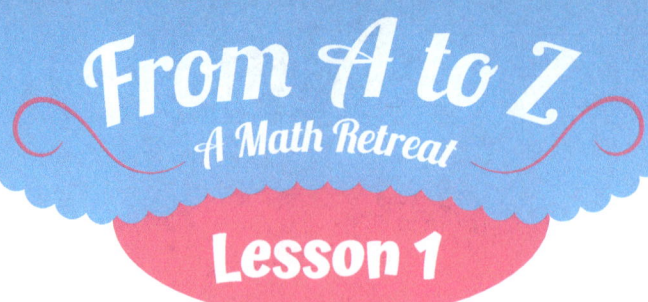

Lesson 1

✎ Solve Each Subtraction Problem

Draw a line through the number of items being taken away. An example has been done for you.

5 - 3 = 2

4 - 2 = ☐

6 - 3 = ☐

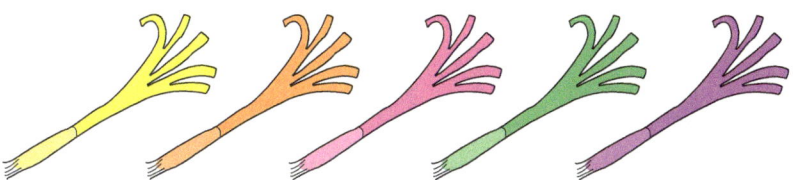   5 - 4 = ☐

10 - 2 = ☐

7 - 2 = ☐

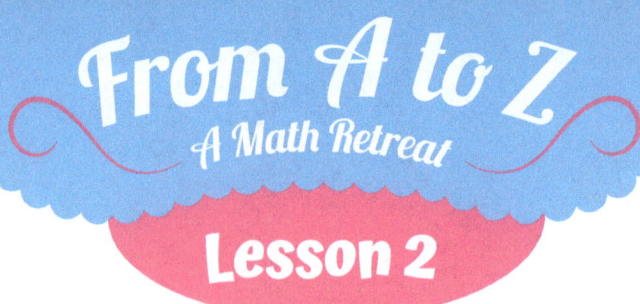

Lesson 2

✏️ **Solve Each Subtraction Problem**

Draw a line through the number of items being taken away.

10 - 7 = ☐

9 - 4 = ☐

5 - 4 = ☐

 7 - 3 = ☐

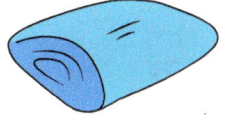 3 - 2 = ☐

 6 - 4 = ☐

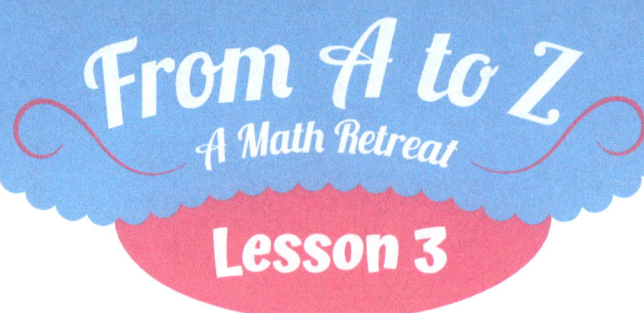

Lesson 3

✏️ Number Line Subtraction

Use the number line to solve the subtraction problems.

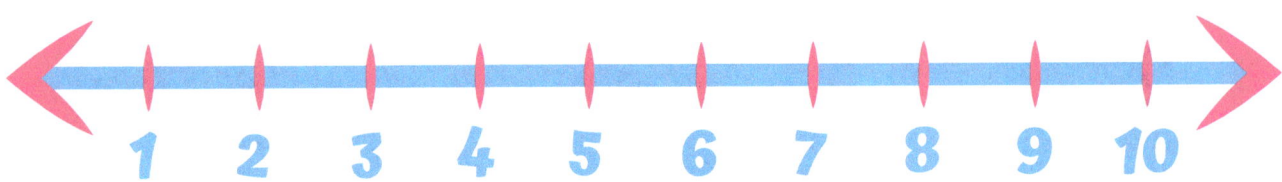

A number line is used to count numbers. You can use a number line to help you subtract. Look at the example below.

Example: 8 - 3

Put your finger on the number eight. Then count back three numbers because you are subtracting by three. Your finger will land on the number five.

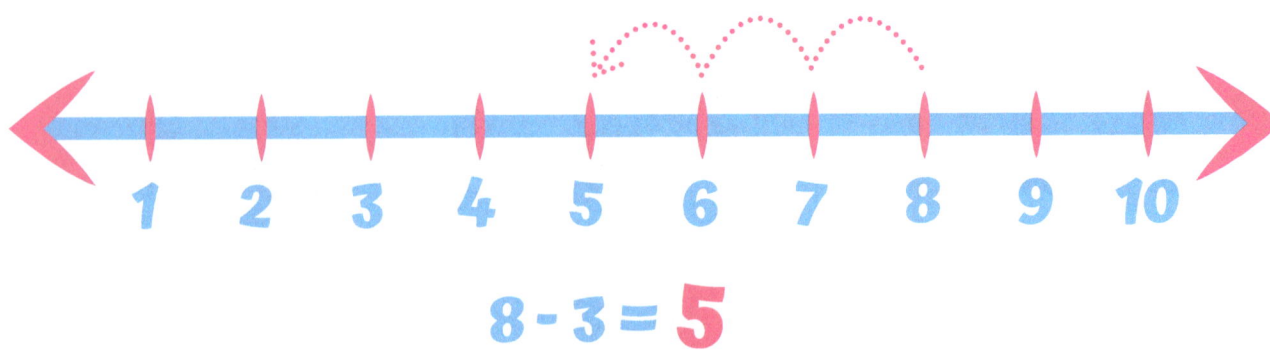

8 - 3 = 5

- 3	- 10	- 6	- 5
7	2	3	5

- 2	- 1	- 6	- 1
1	3	4	1

- 4	- 3	- 4	- 5
2	2	4	1

From A to Z
A Math Retreat
Lesson 4

✏️ **Number Line Subtraction**

Use the number line to solve each problem.

$$\begin{array}{r}8\\-6\\\hline\end{array} \qquad \begin{array}{r}8\\-4\\\hline\end{array} \qquad \begin{array}{r}4\\-4\\\hline\end{array}$$

$$\begin{array}{r}6\\-6\\\hline\end{array} \qquad \begin{array}{r}6\\-2\\\hline\end{array} \qquad \begin{array}{r}3\\-1\\\hline\end{array}$$

$$\begin{array}{r}4\\-3\\\hline\end{array} \qquad \begin{array}{r}9\\-1\\\hline\end{array} \qquad \begin{array}{r}1\\-7\\\hline\end{array}$$

- 7 4	- 8 5	- 10 1

- 5 4	- 8 1	- 8 7

- 6 4	- 3 3	- 9 3

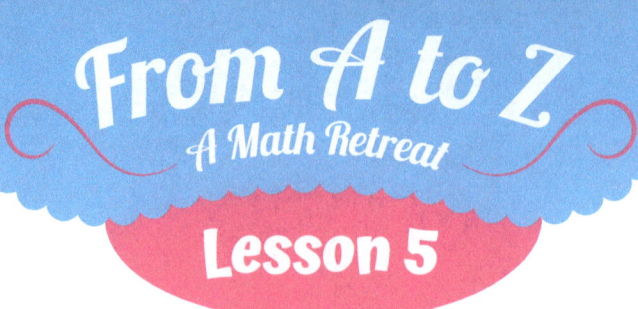

Lesson 5

✏️ Which Equal 6?

Color in the umbrellas that have an answer of 6.

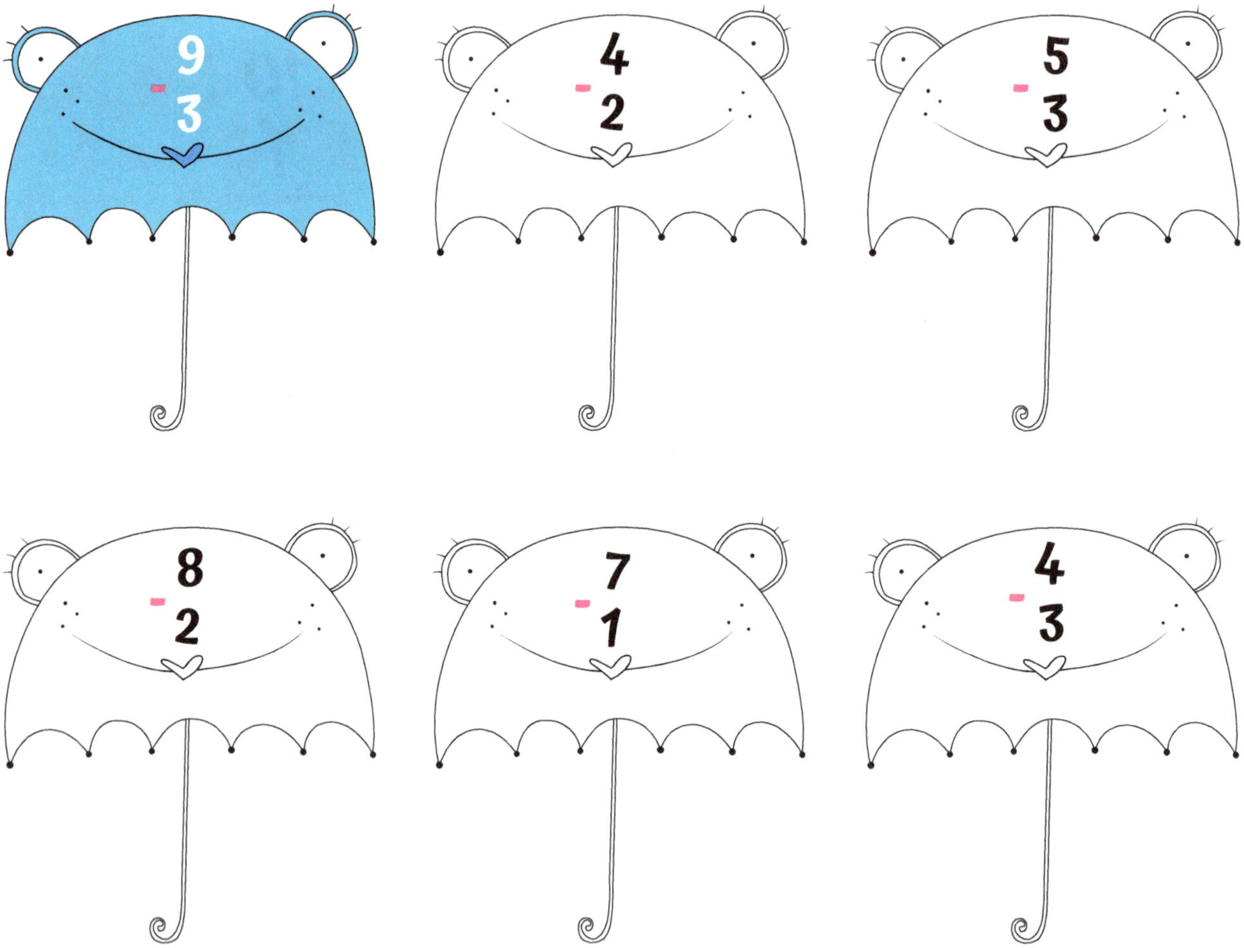

- 9 − 3
- 4 − 2
- 5 − 3
- 8 − 2
- 7 − 1
- 4 − 3

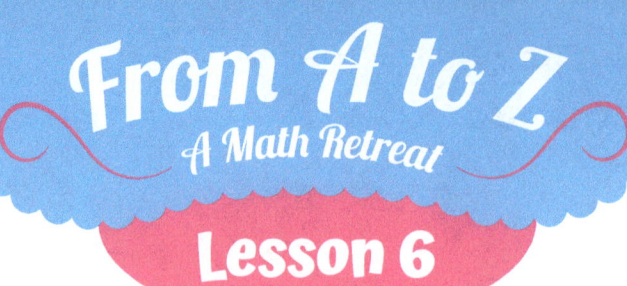

Lesson 6

✏️ Which Equal 2?

Color in the umbrellas that have an answer of 2.

3 − 1

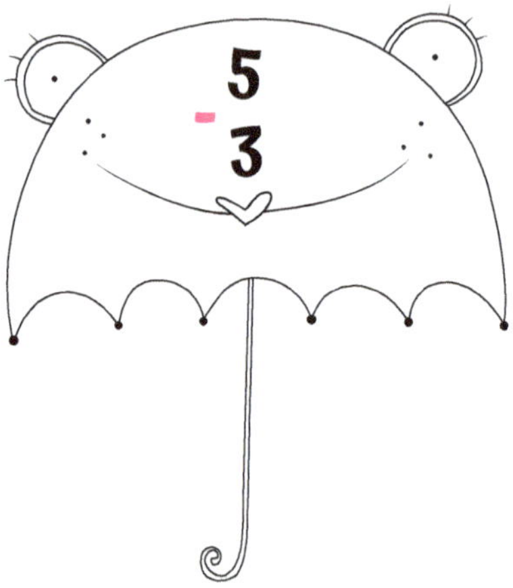

5 − 3

10 − 8

9 − 7

7 − 3

2 − 2

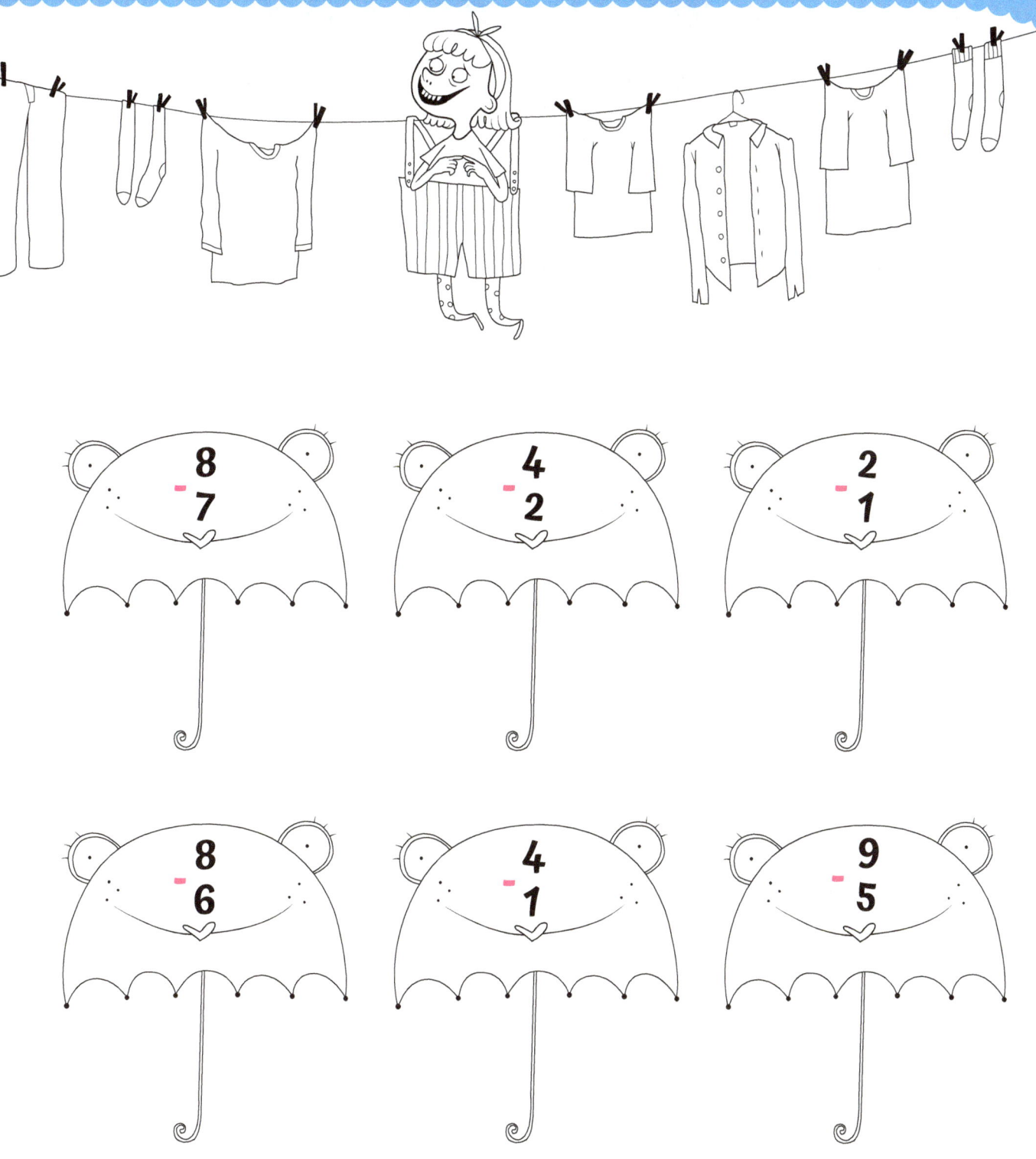

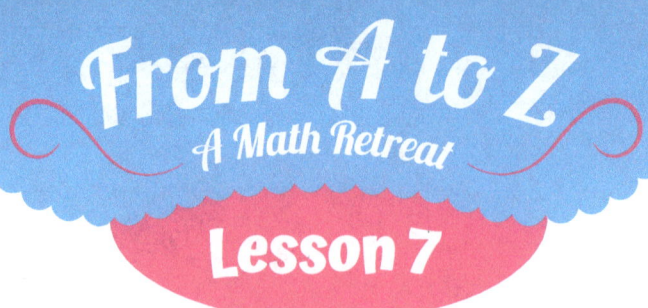

Lesson 7

What's the Answer?

Color in the correct answer for each problem shown.

4 - 2 = ?

| 3 | 1 | 2 |

10 - 5 = ?

| 7 | 8 | 5 |

| 4 | 3 | 2 |

| 4 | 6 | 5 |

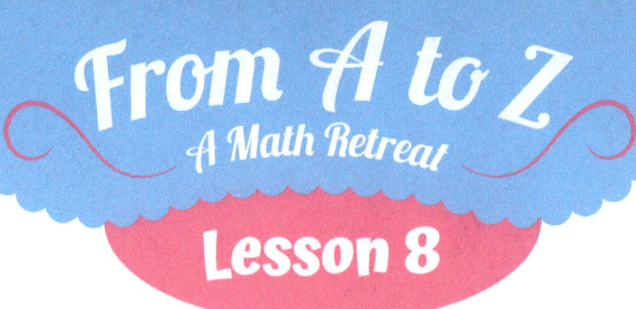

Lesson 8

✏️ **Solve the riddle**

What is Quinn's favorite subject in school?

....
  2   7   5   3   9   4   6

S 7 - 3

G 8 - 3

L 4 - 1

H 9 - 3

E 10 - 8

I 10 - 1

N 9 - 2

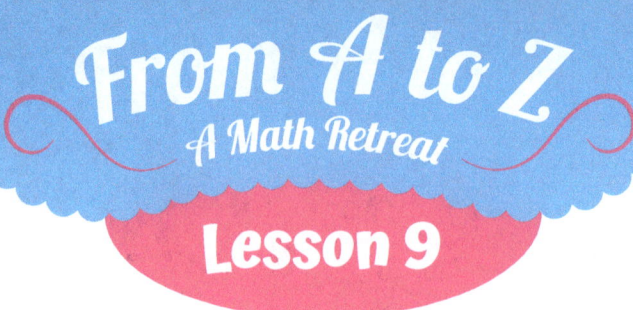

Lesson 9

✎ **Solve the riddle**

Use the sum of each problem to solve the riddle.

....
   3   9   5   4   2   8   5   7   6

T	9 - 3	D	9 - 1
E	10 - 5	R	10 - 1
P	8 - 5	N	8 - 1
S	6 - 2	I	4 - 2

Lesson 10

Solve the riddle

Use the sum of each problem to solve the riddle.

9 − 3 = 6   5 − ☐ = 4

3 − ☐ = 1   8 − ☐ = 6

☐ − 1 = 6   10 − ☐ = 6

9 - ☐ = 4   ☐ - 4 = 3

☐ - 3 = 5   ☐ - 3 = 5

☐ - 2 = 2   5 - ☐ = 3

Congratulations! You're a subtraction master!

You successfully completed your third week of the Jumbo Math lessons.

Go reward yourself with some relaxation time before you start on next week's Math activities.

From A to Z
A Life of Glee

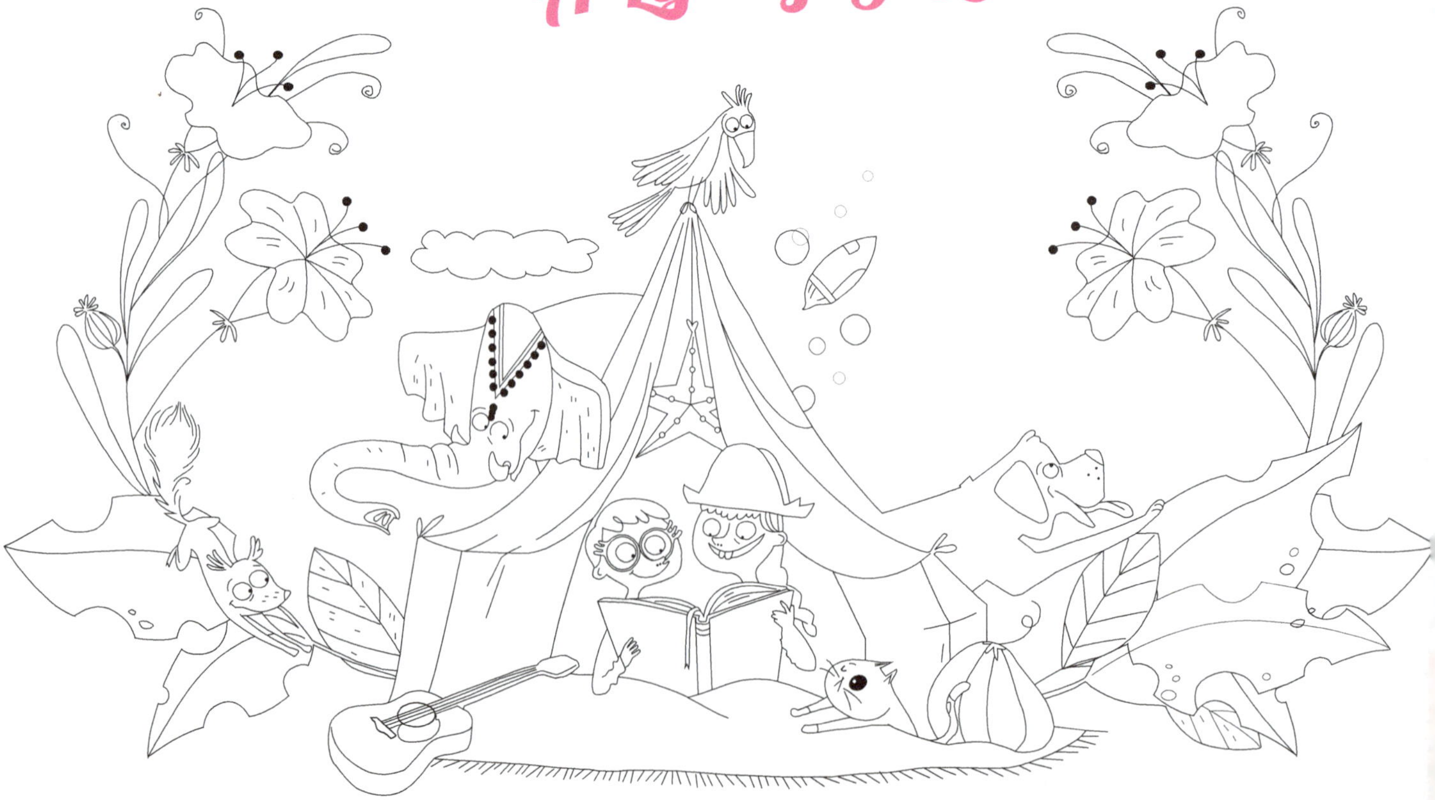

This workbook belongs to:

....

Date Started: **Date Finished:**
....

⭐ Look What I Did ⭐

Mark your progress as you complete each excercise.

Lessons

1	2	3	4	5
6	7	8	9	10

From A to Z

WELCOMES YOU TO

A Math Retreat

(color me)

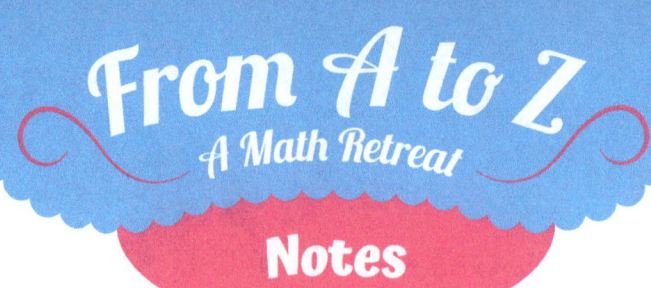

Name: _____
Date: _____

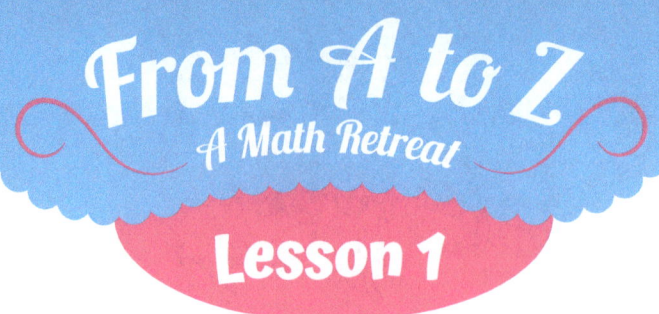

Lesson 1

✎ **Can You Solve It?**

Solve each word problem

Three blue fish are swimming together. One yellow fish joins the group. How many fish are there altogether?

Amber has three green apples. Luke has four red apples. How many apples do they have total?

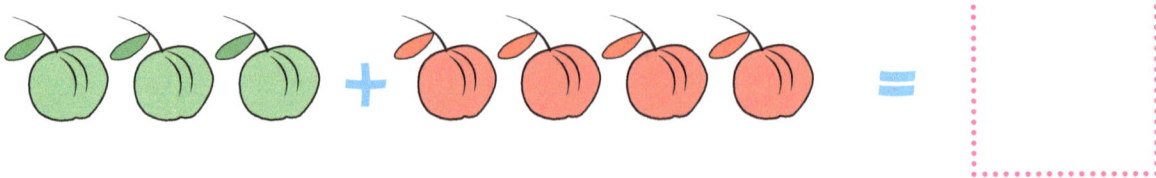

Ricky has four candles on his cake. Ursula has five candles on her cake. What is the total number of candles?

Tammie has three jumping frogs. Her sister has five jumping frogs. How many total frogs are there?

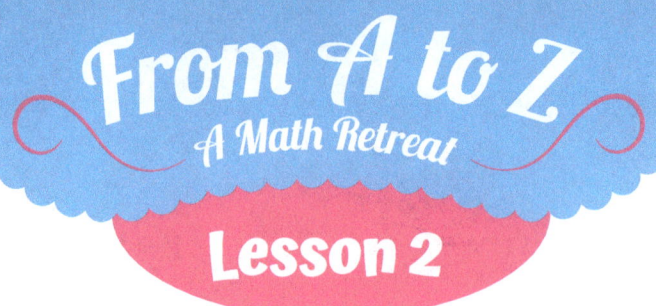

Lesson 2

Can You Solve It?
Solve each word problem

Kristine has five paper hearts. Steve also has five paper hearts.
How many paper hearts do they have in all?

Ellen has three cookies. Xavier gives her six more.
How many cookies does Ellen have altogether?

If Garret has four pink flowers and Yazmin has one yellow flower
How many flowers do they have in all?

Becky has four blue beachballs and Luke has five red beachballs.
How many balls do they have total?

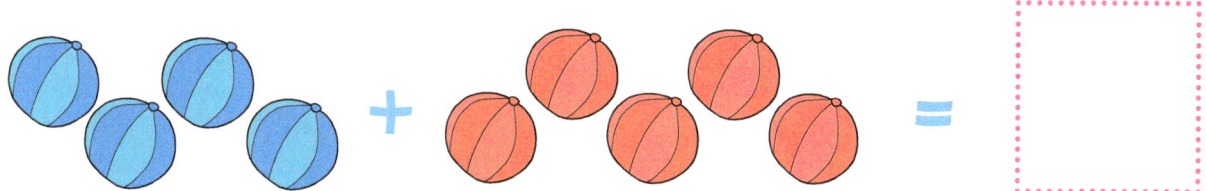

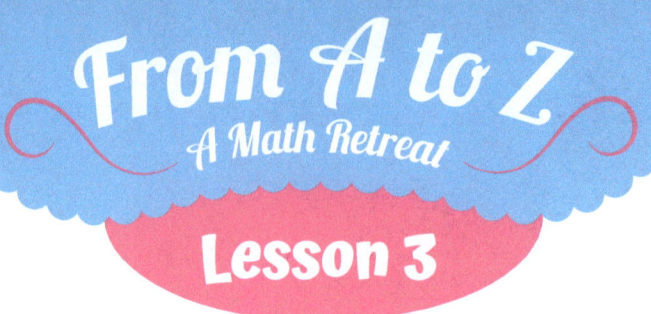

Lesson 3

✎ Can You Solve It?

Solve each word problem

There are four birds chirping. If three birds fly away
How many birds remain?

David has seven donuts. His brother eats two of them.
How many donuts are left?

Ricky has nine guitars. He gives three away.
How many guitars does Ricky have left?

Ambers spots a school of eleven fish. Four of them swim away.
How many fish remain?

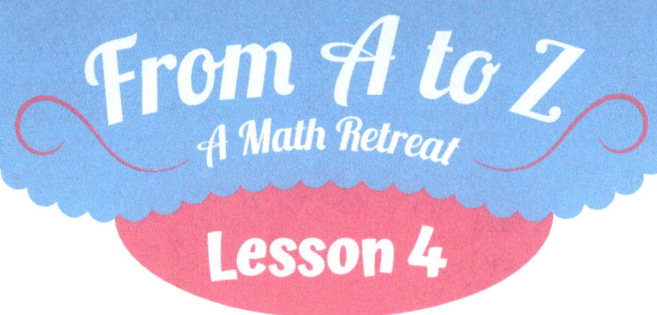

Lesson 4

✏️ Can You Solve It?

Solve each word problem

Winnie has five different t-shirt. She gives two of them away.
How many t-shirt does Winnie have left?

Owen has ten baseball caps. He loses three of them.
How many baseball caps does Owen still have?

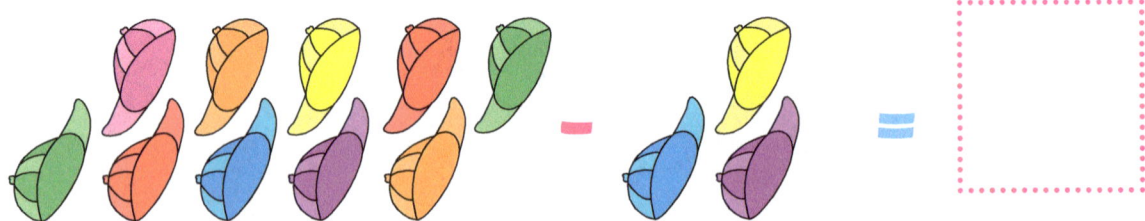

There are five cats and two dogs in the park.
How many more cats are there than dogs?

There are six tomatoes and four apples in a basket.
How many more tomatoes are there than apples?

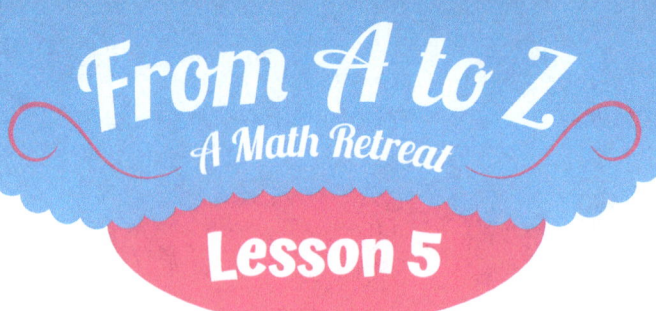

Lesson 5

✏️ Word Problems

Read each addition word problem. Then, draw a picture to go with the word problem. Solve the problem and write your answer in the box.

Yesterday, you had four sprinkle donuts. Today, you bought three more sprinkle donuts. How many donuts do you have altogether?

My Picture

My Answer

You spot four red ships, two blue ships, and three green ships at the harbor. You want to put one flag on each ship. How many flags do you need?

My Picture

My Answer

Lesson 6

✏️ Word Problems

Read each addition word problem. Then, draw a picture to go with the word problem. Solve the problem and write your answer in the box.

Beth and Cody love to run. Beth ran six laps, and Cody ran four. How many laps did Beth and Cody run in all?

My Picture

My Answer

Victoria has six dogs and three cats at home.
How many pets does Victoria have altogether?

My Picture

My Answer

Lesson 7

✎ Word Problems

Read each addition word problem. Then, draw a picture to go with the word problem. Solve the problem and write your answer in the box.

Jackson found eight seashells at the beach. On his walk home, he dropped five of them. How many seashells does Jackson have left?

My Picture

My Answer

You have nine pieces of candy. You give your friend five pieces of candy.
How many pieces of candy do you have left?

My Picture

My Answer

Congratulations!

Give yourself a round of applause.

You successfully completed your Jumbo Math Workbook.

Don't forget to visit us at

www.PuppyDogsAndIceCream.com

for more activities.

If you have any questions, please feel free to email us at:

info@PuppySmiles.org

CPSIA information can be obtained
at www.ICGtesting.com
Printed in the USA
BVHW01s1730130818
524309BV00001B/1/P